OPERATING IN THE COURTS OF HEAVEN TO CLEANSE YOUR BLOODLINE OFFICIAL WORKBOOK

CANCEL THE ENEMY'S CASE AGAINST YOU, YOUR FAMILY, AND YOUR FUTURE

ROBERT HENDERSON

D DESTINY IMAGE

CONTENTS

Introduction   v

1. My Story   1
2. The Lordship of Jesus   8
3. The Reality of Generational Curses   15
4. Covenants Undone   21
5. Why Now?   27
6. Undoing Created Covenants   33
7. Repentance   40
8. Renouncing Covenants   47
9. Give It Back!   54
10. Returning Anything Gained!   60
11. Iniquity Undone   66
12. Iniquity Interruption of God's Will   73
13. The Four Purposes of Iniquity   79
14. Silencing Voices   84
15. Signs of Curses from Our Bloodline   90
16. The Curse of Premature Death   96
17. Revoking Curses That Shorten Lifespans   102
18. From Defendant to Judge   108

About the Publisher   115

INTRODUCTION

Welcome to *Operating in the Courts of Heaven to Cleanse Your Bloodline Official Workbook.* This guide is more than a collection of insights and teachings; it is a transformative journey designed to equip you with the tools and understanding needed to engage in the heavenly realm, address spiritual legalities, and secure the blessings that God has ordained for your life. As you work through these chapters, you will gain a deeper understanding of how iniquities, covenants, and curses from your bloodline can influence your present circumstances and learn how to revoke these legal claims in the Courts of Heaven.

The foundational truth throughout this workbook is that God is a righteous Judge who governs the spiritual and physical realms with justice and mercy. While salvation is freely given through Christ's sacrifice, spiritual legalities may still hinder the manifestation of His promises in your life. These hindrances are often rooted in **bloodline iniquities, generational covenants, and unrepented sins**. By addressing these issues, you position yourself to step into the fullness of your God-given identity and authority.

WHAT YOU CAN EXPECT TO RECEIVE

This workbook is structured to take you through a process of discovery, repentance, and empowerment. Each chapter builds on the last, providing both biblical foundation and practical application. Here's what you can expect as you engage with the material:

1. **Understanding the Spiritual Legal System** The workbook will introduce you to the biblical concept of the Courts of Heaven, highlighting how God's governance operates through legal processes. You will learn that **the enemy's accusations and curses are rooted in legal rights he claims through sin and iniquity**, and you will discover how to counter these accusations using the testimony of Jesus' blood.

2. **Identifying Bloodline Iniquities and Curses** Many of the challenges you face today may stem from unresolved issues in your family's spiritual history. This workbook will guide you in identifying **signs of curses, iniquities, and covenants** that grant the enemy legal access to hinder your life and destiny. You will also learn to discern areas where the enemy's accusations need to be silenced.

3. **Repenting and Revoking Legal Claims** One of the most significant takeaways from this journey is the power of repentance. Through heartfelt prayer and intentional confession, you will address sins and iniquities in your life and lineage. You will learn how to **stand in the gap for your family** and revoke the enemy's legal rights, bringing freedom and restoration.

4. **Embracing Your Authority in the Courts of Heaven** As you cleanse your bloodline, you will transition from the role of a defendant pleading your case to that of a judge in the Courts of Heaven. This shift empowers you to **decree God's will over your life, family, and culture**, aligning your actions with His kingdom purposes.

5. **Breaking Curses and Securing Blessings** The workbook provides step-by-step guidance on breaking curses related to **premature death, poverty, sickness, and spiritual stagnation**. You will also explore how to secure long life, prosperity, and divine favor by aligning with God's promises and plans.

6. **The Role of Prayer and Prophetic Insight** Each chapter emphasizes the importance of prayer as a vehicle for change. You will gain insights into prophetic prayer, understanding how to **partner with the Holy Spirit to influence spiritual outcomes** and align with heaven's agenda.

7. **Walking in Freedom and Purpose** As you progress, you will notice a tangible shift in your spiritual life. The removal of legal hindrances will pave the way for greater intimacy with God, clarity of purpose, and effectiveness in advancing His kingdom. **Freedom from the weight of bloodline iniquities enables you to walk confidently in the promises of God.**

KEY TAKEAWAYS FROM THE MESSAGES

- **Spiritual Legalities Govern the Earthly Realm:** Every challenge or resistance you face may have a spiritual root. Recognizing this truth is the first step toward overcoming.

- **The Blood of Jesus Speaks on Your Behalf**: Jesus' sacrifice is the foundation of your victory. His blood nullifies every accusation when applied with faith and understanding.
- **Repentance is the Key to Freedom**: True transformation begins with repentance, both for your sins and those of your bloodline.
- **Your Identity is Central to Your Authority**: You are not merely a victim of circumstances; you are a king and priest in God's kingdom, called to exercise authority.
- **Blessings Await the Cleansed Bloodline**: When legal hindrances are removed, God's blessings flow freely, bringing restoration, provision, and joy.

HOW TO USE THIS WORKBOOK

This workbook is designed to be both a teaching tool and a practical guide. Each chapter includes:

- **Detailed explanations of spiritual principles and their biblical foundations.**
- **Reflective questions to help you process the material personally.**
- **Actionable steps that guide you in applying the lessons.**
- **Journaling prompts to document your prayers, revelations, and progress.**

Approach each chapter prayerfully and with an open heart. Take time to meditate on the scriptures provided and allow the

Holy Spirit to lead you into deeper understanding and repentance. Engage with the reflective questions and journaling prompts to personalize the material and track your spiritual growth.

MOVING FORWARD

This workbook is not just about gaining knowledge; it is about encountering transformation. As you move through the chapters, you will experience the power of God's Word, the freedom of His forgiveness, and the authority of His promises. By the end of this journey, you will not only have cleansed your bloodline but also stepped into your role as a judge in the Courts of Heaven.

This is your time to break free from limitations, secure God's blessings, and walk boldly in your divine destiny. Let the journey begin!

CHAPTER 1
MY STORY

In the midst of overwhelming challenges, remember that God's grace is sufficient for you, for His power is made perfect in weakness.

2 Corinthians 12:9 (NKJV): "And He said to me, 'My grace is sufficient for you, for My strength is made perfect in weakness.' Therefore most gladly I will rather boast in my infirmities, that the power of Christ may rest upon me."

In this chapter of my journey, I open up about the **Transition to Itinerant Ministry**. After 22 years of fulfilling pastoral duties, my wife Mary and I embraced a new calling that led us away from the familiar comfort of Waco, Texas, to the challenging terrains of Colorado Springs, Colorado. This move, though initially met with a period of success and family reunification as several of our grown children joined us, soon spiraled into a series of unanticipated difficulties. The heart of these challenges stemmed from our vulnerable position as we navigated this significant life change, highlighting the importance of support and stability in ministry roles.

Unexpectedly, we were engulfed by **Slander and Gossip**. This ordeal began when an influential leader publicly endorsed me, akin to the biblical story of Joseph, who received the coat of many colors from his father and faced his brothers' envy and betrayal. The endorsement, rather than fostering unity, ignited hostility and division. Some well-known ministries and individuals, who once stood by this leader, turned against me with ferocity, spreading baseless accusations and attempting to tarnish my reputation. Their actions were a stark reminder of the destructive power of jealousy and the severe impact negative words can have on one's life and ministry.

At the same time, the **Apostolic Authority Challenged** key point became a harsh reality. The pastor I had appointed in Waco began to seek complete control over the church, attempting to diminish my influence and role. His actions, coupled with his wife's illness, garnered sympathy from the congregation, which he leveraged to fuel opposition against me. This struggle within the church underscored the complexities of leadership and the delicate balance required to maintain authority and respect in such a dynamic.

Financial Hardship soon followed, a direct result of the slander and internal church conflicts. The financial support we had relied on was abruptly withdrawn, plunging our family into economic uncertainty. This phase was particularly distressing as it threatened the very stability of our family and ministry, teaching me the painful lesson that financial security can be fleeting, and the importance of having a robust financial plan that does not rely solely on one source or community.

Amid these professional and financial upheavals, personal attacks were also directed towards my family, making the **Personal Attacks on Family** a particularly painful chapter in our lives. My son Adam went through a heart-wrenching divorce, and my son Mark's life was nearly destroyed by drug addiction. These personal crises brought home the stark reality of how public ministry can extend its pressures and trials into the most private areas of one's life, affecting not just the individual but their entire family.

The betrayal reached a peak when I discovered the **Legal and Property Issues** involving the pastor I had trusted in Waco. He had misused his legal authority to secure a loan by putting up my house as collateral, without my knowledge. This act of betrayal not only resulted in financial loss but also a deep sense of personal betrayal and violation, highlighting the necessity of vigilance and explicit clarity in legal and financial dealings.

Throughout these trials, the **Spiritual and Emotional Toll** on myself and my family was considerable. Each day brought with it a weight of emotional and spiritual anguish, raising questions about the reason behind these relentless attacks and the apparent silence of God in our darkest moments. It was a period of profound soul-searching and reliance on faith to sustain us when all else seemed to fail.

It was during this low point that I encountered the transformative teaching of the **Introduction to the Courts of Heaven**. This new spiritual understanding offered me not just insight but practical strategies to address the injustices we were facing. It was a pivotal moment that brought clarity and direction, helping me to see beyond the immediate turmoil and understand the spiritual dimensions of the battles we were engaged in.

This revelation brought with it a renewed sense of **Hope and Deliverance**. I began to see that despite the overwhelming challenges, there was a pathway to recovery and victory. This hope was not just for my own situation but something I could share with others facing similar trials, providing them with the tools and understanding necessary to overcome their own battles.

Lastly, I learned the crucial lesson on **Spiritual Warfare and Legal Rights**. My prayer life deepened as I sought to uncover any legal grounds that the enemy might be using against me and my family. This spiritual strategy emphasized the importance of legal rights in the spiritual realm, guiding me to pray with more focus and authority, seeking to align every aspect of our lives with God's will and legal order in His courts.

Reflective Questions

1. How do transitions in life and ministry expose vulnerabilities? Reflect on how significant changes can both open new opportunities and introduce unexpected challenges.
2. In what ways can jealousy and endorsement impact leadership dynamics? Consider the role of public endorsement in your life and how it has influenced relationships and perceptions.
3. What measures can be taken to ensure financial and operational integrity in leadership roles? Reflect on the importance of transparency and accountability in financial dealings, especially in church or ministry settings.
4. How can personal and familial challenges impact public ministry? Think about the ways personal life can intersect with public roles and the pressures it can create.
5. What role does spiritual understanding play in overcoming life's legal and spiritual challenges? Consider how deepening spiritual insights can provide new strategies for dealing with personal and communal issues.

. . .

ACTIONABLE STEPS

- **Cultivate a Supportive Network**: Build and maintain a network of trusted advisors and friends who can provide support, guidance, and honest feedback during transitions and crises.
- **Equip Yourself with Legal and Financial Knowledge**: Enhance your understanding of legal and financial matters related to your role to protect yourself and your organization from potential mismanagement or fraud.
- **Engage in Regular Spiritual Reflection**: Commit to regular prayer and spiritual reflection to stay aligned with God's purpose and to fortify yourself against spiritual attacks.

JOURNALING Prompt

Reflect on a time when you faced a significant challenge or transition in your life. How did you see God's grace at work in your weakness? What did you learn about His strength in your life during this time?

~

THE LORDSHIP OF JESUS

In the midst of overwhelming challenges, remember that God's grace is sufficient for you, for His power is made perfect in weakness.

2 Corinthians 12:9 (NKJV): "And He said to me, 'My grace is sufficient for you, for My strength is made perfect in weakness.' Therefore most gladly I will rather boast in my infirmities, that the power of Christ may rest upon me."

In the second chapter of my journey, I delve deeper into the profound realizations about the **Foundation on the Rock.** As my family and I navigated through our tribulations, it became evident that our steadfastness was not incidental but the result of a life diligently built on the teachings of Jesus. This realization mirrors the parable of the two houses that Jesus described in Luke 6, where one house withstands the storms due to its solid foundation on the rock, while the other, built on sand, collapses under pressure.

The strength of our spiritual foundation was significantly

enhanced by our commitment to **Authenticity in Faith**. In both our public ministry and private devotion, we maintained a consistent lifestyle that reflected our true faith. This authenticity was vital because, as I've come to understand, discrepancies between public persona and private devotion often lead to spiritual collapse. Living a unified life, devoid of hypocrisy, fortifies the spiritual structure of one's life against inevitable storms.

The parable of the two houses also emphasizes the importance of **Reacting to the Word**. It wasn't enough to merely listen to Jesus' teachings; the true test came in acting upon them. The house that endured the storm was not just a hearer but a doer of the Word. This active response to divine instruction is what separates a life that is merely touched by faith from one that is transformed by it.

Understanding **Jesus as Absolute Lord** as detailed in Philippians 2:8-11 reshaped my perspective of what it means to submit to His authority. Jesus' lordship is rooted in His obedience and surrender to God, which led to His exaltation. This teaches us that our acknowledgment of His lordship should also be reflected in our complete submission to His will, aligning every aspect of our lives with His divine purpose.

The concept of **Active Obedience** plays a crucial role in maintaining our legal standing in the spiritual realm, particularly in the Courts of Heaven. My personal experiences taught me that obedience is more than a spiritual discipline; it is a legal act that establishes our allegiance and authority under Christ's lordship. Each act of obedience fortifies our legal rights and privileges in the spiritual domain.

In line with the teachings of Luke 6, where Jesus emphasizes the need to **Hear and Do**, I have found that this dynamic interaction with the divine word is foundational for building a resilient spiritual life. Each decision to act on Jesus' words reinforces our spiritual structure, enabling us to withstand life's unpredictable challenges.

The **Legal Place Before God** that we occupy can be significantly enhanced through acts of obedience and dedication. For instance, my commitment to supporting educational initiatives for underprivileged girls not only impacted lives in the physical realm but also fortified my standing in the spiritual courts, highlighting the interconnectedness of our spiritual actions and their worldly implications.

The direction to invest in these girls' education was an instance of **Prophetic Obedience**. This obedience was not arbitrary but a direct response to a divine directive, which not only changed their lives but also had profound implications on my spiritual authority and legacy.

Moreover, the idea of **Continuous Building** is essential for anyone seeking to lead a life under Christ's lordship. Just as the Apostle Paul continually strived to grow and improve upon his faith, we too must view our spiritual journey as a continual process of construction, always adding to and reinforcing our faith through constant learning and application.

Finally, understanding the **Judicial Power of Obedience** has been transformative. Our financial contributions and acts of obedience serve as testimonials in the heavenly courts. Scriptures like Hebrews 7:8 illustrate that our tithes and offerings do more than fulfill a command; they testify on our behalf, advocating for our cause in the spiritual realm.

As we proceed through this study, my hope is that these insights encourage you to examine the depth of your own foundation in Christ and inspire you to build not just for the present but for eternity, establishing a legacy of faith that withstands every storm.

REFLECTIVE QUESTIONS

1. How does building your life on Christ's teachings impact your response to life's storms?
2. In what ways can living authentically, both in public and private, safeguard against spiritual failure?
3. How does actively applying Jesus' words in your daily life strengthen your spiritual foundation?
4. What does it mean to truly acknowledge Jesus as Lord in all areas of your life?
5. How can your personal acts of obedience influence your spiritual authority and legal standing in the Courts of Heaven?

ACTIONABLE STEPS

- **Cultivate Continuous Spiritual Growth**: Engage in daily practices that deepen your understanding and application of Jesus' teachings, ensuring your spiritual foundation is continuously strengthened.
- **Equip Yourself with Scriptural Knowledge**: Regularly study the scriptures to understand the depth of Jesus' lordship and the practical implications of living under His authority.
- **Engage in Prophetic Listening and Obedience**: Develop sensitivity to the Holy Spirit's voice through prayer and meditation, and be ready to act on the divine guidance you receive to fulfill God's purposes.

JOURNALING Prompt

Reflect on a situation where you felt your spiritual foundation was being tested. How did your understanding of Jesus as Lord guide your actions and decisions? What lessons did you learn about building on the rock rather than on sand?

CHAPTER 3

THE REALITY OF GENERATIONAL CURSES

Embrace the truth that through Christ, we have the power to break every chain, including generational curses. His victory on the cross has granted us freedom, empowering us to live unburdened by the past.

2 Corinthians 3:17 (NKJV): "Now the Lord is the Spirit; and where the Spirit of the Lord is, there is liberty."

In this chapter, we delve into a topic that continues to generate significant debate among Christians: the reality of **Generational Curses**. Many believers, influenced by what some call a "false grace message," consider the Old Testament—and its teachings on curses—irrelevant today. However, the **Validity of Old Testament Scriptures** cannot be overstated. The early apostles, including Peter, extensively cited the Old Testament to reinforce their teachings about grace. They understood that the scriptures from the Old Testament were foundational to their faith and essential for understanding the continuity of God's message.

The **Integration of Scriptures** from both Testaments is crucial for a full understanding of God's word. Peter's assertion that the Old Testament is a "light that shines in a dark place" until Jesus returns should resonate with us all (2 Peter 1:19). This underscores that the Old Testament remains relevant, providing essential context and depth to the New Testament teachings. In my journey, recognizing the **Generational Curses Recognized** in the Bible as an ongoing concern has been transformative. These curses, described as consequences for the sins of ancestors affecting subsequent generations, find their remedy in the cross of Christ but require our active engagement to fully overcome.

The **Role of the Holy Spirit** is pivotal in applying the work of the cross to our lives, including the breaking of generational curses. The Holy Spirit helps actualize the legal victories won by Jesus, ensuring these victories manifest in our lives. Understanding the **Legal Aspects of Christ's Work** on the cross shows us that His sacrifice was not only about salvation but also about legally defeating the powers of darkness that include the rights held by generational curses over our lives.

The need for **Active Engagement with Scripture** is paramount, especially in how we apply biblical truths to our lives. As Paul instructed Timothy, we must "rightly divide the word of truth" (2 Timothy 2:15), which involves making careful distinctions within the Scriptures to apply their truths correctly, particularly concerning generational blessings and curses.

The **Relevance of Generational Teachings Today** is clear when we understand that the legal and spiritual principles discussed in the Bible have practical implications for us today. To effectively address generational curses, **Repentance and Legal Action** in the spiritual realm are necessary. This means actively renouncing these curses and any legal ground they may claim, a principle supported by scriptural examples where legal terms are frequently used to describe Christ's redemptive work.

The **Empowerment to Overcome Curses** through Christ is a powerful truth that we hold. By understanding and invoking the legal groundwork laid by His sacrifice, we can confront and annul any generational curses affecting our families. Our redemption through Christ is indeed **Comprehensive Application of Redemption**, which means it addresses every aspect of our lives, offering us complete freedom from past bonds, including generational curses.

By embracing these truths and applying them through faith and the guidance of the Holy Spirit, we can experience the full liberty that Christ intended for us. This journey requires us to be diligent in studying the Scriptures, both Old and New Testaments, to fully grasp and apply their truths. As we do this, we not only enhance our understanding but also ensure that our lives and those of our descendants are free from the bonds of the past, enabling us to live out the full potential God has for us in Christ.

REFLECTIVE QUESTIONS

1. How does understanding the continuity between the Old and New Testaments enhance your approach to biblical teachings on generational curses?
2. In what ways can the Holy Spirit's role in applying Christ's work on the cross be more actively sought in your life to address issues like generational curses?
3. What steps can you take to better understand and apply the legal aspects of redemption Christ has provided, especially concerning generational curses?
4. How does repentance play a role in dealing with generational sins and their effects on your life?
5. What are practical ways you can invoke the

comprehensive application of redemption in areas of your life affected by generational curses?

ACTIONABLE STEPS

- **Cultivate a Deeper Understanding of Scripture**: Engage in regular study of both the Old and New Testaments to grasp the full narrative of Scripture and its application to issues like generational curses.
- **Equip Yourself with Knowledge on Spiritual Legal Rights**: Learn about the legal aspects of Christ's work on the cross and how these can be applied through the Holy Spirit to break generational curses.
- **Engage in Regular Repentance and Legal Spiritual Actions**: Regularly repent for any known sins and engage in prayer that specifically addresses revoking any legal rights or curses that may be impacting your generational line.

JOURNALING Prompt

Reflect on any patterns or struggles in your family that might be indicative of generational curses. How can you apply the truths of Scripture and the power of the Holy Spirit to break these patterns and experience the full freedom Christ has won for you?

CHAPTER 4
COVENANTS UNDONE

Through Christ, we have the power to renounce old covenants and reclaim our spiritual heritage, ensuring that our lives are not defined by past agreements but by our current covenant with Him.

Hebrews 12:24 (NKJV): "To Jesus the Mediator of the new covenant, and to the blood of sprinkling that speaks better things than that of Abel."

In Chapter 4, I share a critical juncture in my spiritual journey, where despite **Enduring Attacks Under Christ's Lordship**, my family and I found ourselves grappling with unrelenting spiritual warfare. This period was marked by an intense feeling of helplessness as **Ineffectiveness of Previous Spiritual Practices** that once brought victory now seemed futile. Everything I had learned and applied from my deep-rooted prayer life since 1980 appeared to lose its potency. This drastic change pushed me towards seeking a deeper, perhaps previously unexplored, spiritual intervention.

During this challenging time, an **Unexpected Invitation and Revelation** came my way. I was invited to minister in a foreign country, an invitation that was about to unveil profound spiritual insights. It was here that I first encountered the concept of **Bloodline Cleansing**. Initially, I was skeptical and unaware of what this meant or its necessity. However, as the ministry leader explained the potential for legal grounds in my bloodline giving demons and principalities the right to attack, I realized the gravity of what I was dealing with.

As I delved into this new understanding, it became evident that an **Encounter with Generational Covenants** was at play. A prophetic individual during the session revealed that an ancestor had made a covenant with a demonic entity known as Parax. This was a pivotal moment for me; the realization that there were **Spiritual Warfare and Legal Grounds** affecting my life was both shocking and enlightening. The notion that my struggles might have a generational component rooted in spiritual legality prompted me to take immediate action.

The process of **Renouncing Old Covenants** was intense and deeply spiritual. Guided by the ministry team, I prayed to renounce any agreements made by my ancestors with dark forces, explicitly breaking away from these ties in the name of Jesus. The **Immediate Impact of Spiritual Actions** was astonishing. I felt a shift in the spiritual atmosphere, a clear sign that significant spiritual chains had been broken. This session marked a turning point, highlighting the **Long-Term Implications of Spiritual Deliverance** on my life and ministry.

Reflecting on these events has solidified my understanding of the importance of **Integration of Spiritual Deliverance in Daily Life**. It's crucial not only to seek deliverance but to maintain it through continuous spiritual vigilance and practice. This experience has taught me the necessity of incorporating deliverance into regular spiritual disciplines, ensuring that I and my family live free from the burdens that once held us back.

This chapter is a testament to the power of deliverance and the importance of understanding the spiritual legacies we carry. It serves as a reminder that our battles are not always visible and that the spiritual realm holds significant influence over our lives. Through Christ, we have the authority to break every chain, but we must be proactive in seeking and maintaining our spiritual freedom.

REFLECTIVE QUESTIONS

1. How can understanding the role of spiritual attacks help us better prepare for unforeseen challenges in our spiritual journey?
2. What steps can you take when traditional spiritual practices seem ineffective?
3. How can the concept of bloodline cleansing be integrated respectfully and effectively into a broader Christian practice?
4. What are the implications of recognizing and renouncing generational covenants for your personal and family life?
5. How can prophetic insights be responsibly used to guide spiritual warfare and deliverance?

ACTIONABLE STEPS

- **Cultivate Awareness of Spiritual Heritage:** Regularly assess any potential generational issues that might be affecting your spiritual life, seeking guidance and revelation through prayer and fasting.

- **Equip Yourself with Knowledge of Spiritual Warfare**: Educate yourself on the concepts of legal rights in the spiritual realm and how to effectively counteract these through scriptural promises and prayer.

- **Engage in Regular Deliverance Practices**: Implement routine spiritual check-ups and cleansing sessions, either individually or with trusted spiritual leaders, to maintain spiritual health and freedom.

Journaling **Prompt**

Reflect on any areas of your life where you feel recurring challenges or unexplained struggles. Consider how understanding spiritual legacies and applying bloodline cleansing might change your approach to these issues. How can you incorporate these insights into your regular spiritual disciplines?

WHY NOW?

Embrace the understanding that even as challenges arise, they serve as opportunities to reaffirm our covenant with Christ and remove any legal grounds the enemy may claim.

Romans 8:37 (NKJV): "Yet in all these things we are more than conquerors through Him who loved us."

In Chapter 5, titled "Why Now?", I explore a turning point in my life that followed a significant spiritual intervention. The chapter delves into how **Sudden Changes and Deliverance** marked a distinct before and after in my ministry and personal life. This swift transformation was not coincidental but a direct result of addressing and resolving specific spiritual legalities that had given the enemy undue influence over my life.

As I reflect on the series of events that led to this newfound peace and prosperity, I am drawn to consider **Understanding the Timing of Attacks**. It became evident that the increase in spiritual attacks was linked to my decision to step into a broader kingdom role. This role, as revealed during moments of intercession, was pre-ordained and recorded in **Significant of Spiritual Books in Heaven**. These heavenly books contain the blueprints of our destinies, and as such, are integral to understanding the purpose of our lives.

The role of **Intercession and Opening of Spiritual Books** cannot be understated. It is through our fervent prayer and spiritual engagement that these books are accessed, revealing the paths God has laid out for us. This process was transformative for me, bringing to light not just the nature of the attacks I was facing but also the divine strategy for overcoming them. This revelation came through a prophetic insight where I was told, "You will disciple nations." This directive was not just a random statement but a specific calling pulled from the pages of my heavenly book, emphasizing the **Role of Prophetic Revelation in Understanding Destiny**.

However, the journey was not without its challenges. The discovery of a demonic covenant linked to my ancestry—a legal ground that had allowed significant disruption in my life—highlighted the **Impact of Legal Rights on Personal and Ministry Life**. The **Strategic Nature of Spiritual Warfare** became a central theme of my teachings and personal practice, underscoring the importance of not only understanding but actively dismantling these legal footholds.

The Power of Renouncing and Reclaiming our spiritual authority is a critical step toward freedom. This process involves not only identifying and renouncing past agreements made by ourselves or our ancestors but also proactively reclaiming the authority that Christ has established for us through His victory. The immediate and profound changes that followed this spiritual realignment confirmed the effectiveness of these actions.

As I continued to walk in this newfound freedom, the importance of **Continued Vigilance in Spiritual Warfare** became clear. The battles may change in nature, but they do not cease.

Our role is to remain vigilant, constantly seeking to understand and counteract the enemy's plans. This ongoing battle underscores the **Integration of Spiritual Revelations into Ministry**, where my experiences and the insights gained from them form a foundational component of my teachings.

These concepts have not only shaped my ministry but have also offered a roadmap for others facing similar spiritual challenges. The integration of these teachings into daily spiritual practice ensures that we not only face our battles equipped but also pass on this critical knowledge to others in the body of Christ.

Reflecting on this journey, it becomes evident that each challenge faced was an opportunity to delve deeper into the spiritual realm, understanding the legalistic frameworks that influence the natural world. Each victory not only brought personal peace but also equipped me with the tools and understanding to aid others in their spiritual battles, fulfilling the destiny inscribed in my heavenly book and contributing to the broader kingdom impact.

REFLECTIVE QUESTIONS

1. What does the sudden cessation of spiritual attacks in your life tell you about the power of addressing legal rights in the spiritual realm?
2. How can understanding the timing and nature of spiritual attacks help you better prepare for and engage in spiritual warfare?
3. In what ways can you actively seek to understand and fulfill the writings in your heavenly book?
4. How does the concept of heavenly books and their

significance affect your perspective on destiny and purpose?

5. What steps can you take to ensure that you are both reclaiming your spiritual authority and maintaining vigilance against future attacks?

ACTIONABLE STEPS

- **Cultivate a Deeper Understanding of Spiritual Legalities**: Engage in regular study and meditation on scriptures that reveal the nature of spiritual legalities and our authority over them.
- **Equip Yourself with Tools for Spiritual Warfare**: Participate in workshops, seminars, or courses that focus on understanding and practicing spiritual warfare, particularly those that address legal rights and intercession.
- **Engage in Routine Spiritual Maintenance**: Regularly schedule times for personal and corporate intercession to address and pray over any potential legal grounds or spiritual attacks that could impede your God-given destiny.

JOURNALING Prompt

Reflect on any recent spiritual battles or breakthroughs in your life. Consider how understanding the concept of heavenly books and legal rights might have influenced these events. How can this insight shape your approach to future spiritual challenges and opportunities for growth?

CHAPTER 6
UNDOING CREATED COVENANTS

Remember, Christ has overcome the world and all the powers of darkness. Through His sacrifice, we have the victory over every demonic covenant that seeks to bind us. Stand firm in the truth of His Word and the power of His redemption.

2 Corinthians 5:21 (NKJV) - "For He made Him who knew no sin to be sin for us, that we might become the righteousness of God in Him."

As we journey through the concept of **Undoing Created Covenants**, it's crucial to grasp the nature of the spiritual battles we face, particularly those involving demonic covenants. These agreements with devilish powers can significantly impact our lives and those of our descendants. Often formed in times of desperation or ignorance, these covenants can provide a false sense of security or benefit, much like the leaders of Israel in Isaiah 28:14-15, who entered into a covenant with death and Sheol for protection against calamities.

The **Biblical Context of Covenants** deepens our understanding of these spiritual agreements. Covenants are serious commitments and can be formed with both divine and demonic entities. For example, Abraham's interactions with Abimelech over water rights illustrate how covenants can involve tangible trades, such as livestock, to seal agreements (Genesis 21:27-32). These biblical examples show us that covenants have been a method of establishing peace and order but can also lead to spiritual bondage when made with the wrong entities.

The notion of **The Nature of Trades in Spiritual Realms** is exemplified in the scriptures. Not all trading is material; it's a profound spiritual activity as well. Even Lucifer, before his fall, engaged in trading that became corrupted due to his iniquity (Ezekiel 28:14-16). This corruption transformed what was a heavenly function into a manipulative act that ultimately led to his expulsion from God's holy presence.

Jesus' Redemptive Trades serve as the ultimate counteraction to demonic agreements. On the cross, Christ made the most significant trade—His life for our redemption. He took upon Himself our sins so that we might become the righteousness of God (2 Corinthians 5:21). Furthermore, He bore our sicknesses and carried our pains (Isaiah 53:4), trading His divine health for our healing. This sacrificial act broke the chains of poverty, allowing us to claim prosperity (2 Corinthians 8:9).

Through understanding these trades, we learn how we can **Dismantle Demonic Covenants through Christ**. By aligning ourselves with the victory of Jesus' sacrifice, we can renounce and reverse the agreements made by us or our forebears with demonic entities, effectively claiming back our spiritual inheritance.

The concept of **Legal Grounds in the Spiritual Realm** teaches us that both blessings and curses operate under spiritual laws. Just as earthly contracts need legal standing to be enforced, spiritual covenants require spiritual legality, which Jesus' sacrifice provides the basis to contest and overturn.

This leads us to the **Power of Repentance and Renunciation**, crucial steps in dissociating from past demonic covenants. By confessing and forsaking these old agreements, we invoke the power of Christ's atonement to cleanse and free us from any claims those covenants had over our lives.

In exploring **Jesus as the Model of Spiritual Authority**, we see a life that exemplifies God's intention for abundance and provision. Contrary to some teachings, Jesus was not a figure of poverty but managed resources that supported His ministry and those associated with Him. This correct understanding can shift our mindset towards God's provision.

Furthermore, correcting **Misconceptions About Poverty and Wealth** helps us grasp that spiritual abundance is a kingdom principle. Jesus' earthly life, supported by the wise men's gifts and His management of ministry resources, illustrates that God does not glorify poverty but provides abundantly for His purposes.

Finally, the application of the **Applying the Cross's Victory** in our lives involves more than acknowledgment—it requires active engagement. By asserting the truths of Christ's victory in prayer and daily life, we confront and overcome the spiritual forces attempting to thwart God's plans for us.

REFLECTIVE QUESTIONS

1. What are some ways that demonic covenants could have formed unknowingly in your life or your family's history?
2. How can understanding the biblical concept of trades

and covenants deepen your approach to spiritual warfare?

3. In what areas of your life do you need to claim the trade of righteousness, healing, and prosperity made by Jesus on the cross?

4. How can the examples of Jesus' resource management influence your views on God's provision and the handling of finances in your life?

5. What steps can you take to more actively engage in spiritual battles, particularly in renouncing and overturning demonic covenants?

ACTIONABLE STEPS

- **Cultivate an Understanding of Spiritual Legality**: Educate yourself on biblical teachings about covenants and spiritual laws to understand how they impact your spiritual walk and the legal ground they may provide to demonic forces.

- **Equip Yourself with the Word**: Regularly study and meditate on scriptures related to Christ's redemptive work on the cross, focusing on the aspects of trading sin for righteousness, sickness for health, and poverty for prosperity.

- **Engage in Spiritual Warfare**: Actively pray against and renounce any demonic covenants or trades made by you or your ancestors, using the authority of Jesus Christ and the guidance of the Holy Spirit to claim freedom and blessings rightfully yours through Christ.

. . .

JOURNALING Prompt

Reflect on any areas in your life where you might have unknowingly made agreements that are not in line with God's will. Journal about the steps you can take to uncover, renounce, and reverse these agreements, seeking freedom through the power of Jesus' sacrifice.

CHAPTER 7
REPENTANCE

Remember, Christ has overcome the world and all the powers of darkness. Through His sacrifice, we have the victory over every demonic covenant that seeks to bind us. Stand firm in the truth of His Word and the power of His redemption.

2 Corinthians 5:21 (NKJV) - "For He made Him who knew no sin to be sin for us, that we might become the righteousness of God in Him."

As we delve deeper into the spiritual warfare that surrounds us, it's imperative to recognize the profound implications of our actions on the spiritual realm. The primary **Understanding the Devil's Motive** is not a mere disruption of our peace or happiness, but a strategic delay of his inevitable judgment as prophesied in Revelation. He knows that each step we take in God's will hastens his demise, and thus, he targets us vigorously.

It's fascinating yet sobering to realize that our spiritual engagements can influence timelines of eschatological events.

The **Connection Between Our Actions and Satan's Judgment** is more direct than we often perceive. According to Hebrews, as the Church fulfills its God-given mandate, it propels history towards the culmination of God's plan, including Satan's judgment. Our active engagement in fulfilling divine mandates can indeed **Hasten the Day of the Lord**, echoing the message of 2 Peter that our pursuit of holiness and godliness can accelerate the return of Christ and the ultimate defeat of evil.

Satan's Strategy Against Our Destiny involves a meticulous examination of our lives and lineages to find any breach through which he can legally obstruct our spiritual progress. He is well aware that each believer is on a divine assignment, etched in the books of heaven, as described in Psalms. Our purpose is not just written for us to lead content lives but to actively thwart Satan's reign by aligning with God's redemptive agenda.

As believers, we are God's workmanship, created for significant acts preordained by God Himself. Fulfilling these, which Ephesians highlights, pushes forward the **Power of Our Preordained Purpose**. Our concerted efforts bring us closer to the resolution of the **Mystery of God**, which is the complete realization of His redemptive plan. Conversely, the **Mystery of Iniquity** or lawlessness actively works to counter God's purposes, underscoring a cosmic battle outlined in 2 Thessalonians where every act of sin or lawlessness on our part fuels the enemy's agenda.

In the face of such overwhelming cosmic forces, the weapon of **Repentance as a Strategic Weapon** is more potent than ever perceived. Genuine repentance, turning away from sin and realigning with God's will, effectively annuls the legal footholds Satan claims over our lives. This action restores our spiritual authority, giving us the leverage to break generational curses and demonic strongholds, thereby allowing us to live out our divine destinies.

Moreover, the act of repentance not only affects our spiritual standing but also enhances our **Impact of Repentance on Our Spiritual Authority**. Each act of turning away from sin and embracing God's ways dismantles the enemy's plans and accelerates the fulfillment of God's kingdom on earth.

The efficacy of Jesus' sacrifice on the cross cannot be overstated, particularly when discussing spiritual legality. The **Role of the Blood of Jesus** in our lives speaks of better things than the blood of Abel—it speaks of mercy, forgiveness, and restoration instead of vengeance. This powerful advocacy enables us to stand in the courts of heaven with confidence, contesting every accusation brought against us by the enemy.

Lastly, the **Legal and Relational Dynamics of Confession** secure our forgiveness and cleansing from sin. True confession aligns us with God's perspective, enabling us to speak with authority against the accusations of the enemy, thereby fortifying our spiritual defenses.

Understanding these dynamics transforms how we engage in spiritual warfare, pray, and live out our faith daily. By harnessing the truths of our spiritual authority and the power of repentance, we not only secure our personal victories but also contribute to the larger narrative of God's eternal plan. As we move forward, let us do so with a renewed commitment to live intentionally, aware that our actions in the spiritual realm have far-reaching consequences.

REFLECTIVE QUESTIONS

1. How can recognizing the devil's ultimate motive change your daily approach to spiritual life and warfare?
2. In what ways can you actively participate in

hastening the return of Christ according to 2 Peter 3:11-12?

3. What specific areas of your life might Satan be targeting due to legal rights gained through your bloodline?

4. How can you incorporate regular, heartfelt repentance into your spiritual routine to maintain freedom from demonic influences?

5. What steps can you take to ensure your confession aligns with God's view of sin, thus enhancing its effectiveness in the spiritual realm?

ACTIONABLE STEPS

- **Cultivate Awareness of Spiritual Timelines**: Educate yourself and your community about the direct impact of your spiritual life on hastening the return of Christ and the judgment of Satan. Use this knowledge to motivate a more disciplined and fervent spiritual life.

- **Equip with Knowledge of Bloodline Rights**: Learn about the ways in which legal rights might be granted to demonic forces through generational sins. Engage in prayer and fasting to receive revelation on breaking these legal grounds.

- **Engage in Consistent Repentance and Confession**: Establish a routine of deep, personal repentance and confession. Make it a regular practice to confess not only personal sins but also to seek revelation on ancestral sins that may affect your spiritual authority.

. . .

JOURNALING Prompt

Reflect on the role of repentance in your spiritual life. How often do you find yourself truly repenting in a way that aligns with God's desires? Journal about your experiences with repentance and any insights you gain from praying about your and your family's historical sins. Consider how this practice can deepen your relationship with God and increase your spiritual authority.

REPENTANCE

CHAPTER 8

RENOUNCING COVENANTS

Be empowered by the victory Christ has won for us. Stand firm, knowing that His triumph over the enemy grants us the freedom to renounce any ties that bind us to darkness. Embrace the liberty you've been given through His sacrifice.

James 4:7 (NKJV) - "Therefore submit to God. Resist the devil and he will flee from you."

As we progress through our spiritual journey, understanding how to effectively break away from demonic influences is crucial. It is vital to not only repent for past sins but also to actively **renounce any covenants with demonic forces**. This chapter delves into the **Importance of Renouncing Covenants**, emphasizing that post-repentance, our verbal declarations play a pivotal role in severing ties with these malevolent powers. By using our words to declare our separation, we wield our God-given authority to nullify these demonic covenants, echoing the scriptural example where Paul **renounced shameful and deceitful practices.**

In 2 Corinthians 4:1-2, Paul's renouncement of hidden, shameful things highlights the transformative power of bringing darkness into light, which we too can apply to our spiritual battles. This reflects not only a rejection of past misdeeds but also a decisive step towards transparency and integrity. When we declare out loud that we **renounce demonic agreements**, we use the **Power of Words in the Spiritual Realm** to solidify our stance in the sight of God and the spiritual witnesses. This act is not just symbolic but carries significant spiritual weight, altering our standing and alignments in the unseen world.

Moreover, **Scriptural Basis for Renouncing** provides us with a foundational understanding that our walk with God should be devoid of deceit and manipulation, instead characterized by the manifestation of truth. This truth not only sets us free but also empowers us to stand firm against demonic strategies aimed at our downfall. Through renunciation, we exercise our **Spiritual Authority**, which involves more than just speaking words; it is an assertion of our dominion over the forces that seek to enslave us.

Persistent prayer and proclamation, as demonstrated by Daniel in the scriptures, reveal that our words do indeed reach the heavens and precipitate spiritual activity. Daniel's steadfastness in prayer brought about angelic intervention, demonstrating the **Impact of Persistent Prayer**. This persistence is crucial, as it teaches us that despite delays or seeming silence from the heavenly realms, our prayers are effective from the moment they are uttered. Just like Daniel, we should maintain our spiritual disciplines, knowing that our **Words Summon Spiritual Powers**, a truth that should encourage us to continue in faith without wavering.

The legal aspects of spiritual warfare, particularly **The Legal Aspects of Binding and Loosing**, are foundational to understanding how we can enact God's will on earth as it is in heaven.

With the keys of the kingdom, we have the authority to bind demonic forces and loose God's plans and purposes in our lives. This authority is not arbitrary but is anchored in the divine legal system, where our words align with God's laws to enforce the victory Christ achieved on the cross.

To fully wield this authority, we must ensure that all **Legal Rights of Demons** are revoked. This involves thorough spiritual housekeeping to ensure there are no lingering legal footholds from our past or our family lineage that the enemy could use against us. Each act of renunciation should be seen as a strategic **Use of Spiritual Tools**, where we declare our freedom and enforce the enemy's defeat.

Finally, ensuring that these declarations are not made in vain requires us to **Ensure Legal Grounds Are Cleared** in the spiritual realm. This safeguard prevents potential backlash from the enemy, fortifying our spiritual defenses and ensuring that our declarations of freedom are not only heard but are legally binding. This thorough approach ensures that our efforts to live out our God-given destinies are not hindered by unresolved spiritual liabilities.

In essence, the process of renouncing demonic covenants is integral to walking in the fullness of freedom Christ has purchased for us. Each step, from understanding our authority to effectively utilizing it, is crucial in maintaining our victory over the enemy. Let us, therefore, approach our spiritual duties with diligence, faith, and the wisdom that God provides, ensuring that every word we speak in renunciation is backed by the authority of heaven and is effective in enforcing the kingdom of God in our lives.

REFLECTIVE QUESTIONS

1. What are some demonic covenants or agreements you might need to renounce to experience greater spiritual freedom?
2. How can you more effectively use your words to exercise spiritual authority in your life?
3. What steps can you take to ensure that you are not just repenting but also actively renouncing any demonic influences?
4. In what ways can you incorporate persistent prayer into your daily routine to mirror the perseverance of biblical figures like Daniel?
5. How can you educate yourself more about the legal aspects of spiritual warfare to better engage in binding and loosing?

ACTIONABLE STEPS

- **Cultivate a Deeper Understanding of Spiritual Authority**: Study biblical teachings and resources that explain the power of words and spiritual authority so that you can more effectively engage in renouncing demonic covenants.
- **Equip Yourself Through Persistent Prayer**: Develop a daily prayer routine that includes specific times dedicated to renouncing, binding, and loosing, thus building your spiritual resilience and authority.
- **Engage in Regular Spiritual Check-ups**: Regularly examine your life and lineage for any potential legal

rights or openings that may need to be addressed to maintain your spiritual health and authority.

JOURNALING **Prompt**

Reflect on any specific areas in your life where you might need to renounce agreements or covenants. Consider how these ties have influenced your spiritual journey and write down a declaration of renunciation for each, committing to walk in the truth and freedom God provides.

CHAPTER 9
GIVE IT BACK!

Trust in God's provision, for it is through this trust that we find the courage to give back anything not meant for us. His goodness ensures that what we relinquish, when done in obedience, will be replaced with greater, purer gifts from above.

James 1:17 Every good gift and every perfect gift is from above, and comes down from the Father of lights, with whom there is no variation or shadow of turning.

In our spiritual walk, it is vital to **recognize the true source of our blessings.** Often, we encounter situations where, out of need or desperation, we might unknowingly enter agreements that bind us to dark powers. These covenants promise gain but at the cost of our spiritual freedom. The path to true freedom involves the **willingness to relinquish these ill-gotten gains**, which, though seemingly beneficial, tether us to the demonic.

Understanding that **every good and perfect gift comes from above** helps reinforce our resolve to sever these unholy ties. It is not just about renouncing the gains but also about a profound acknowledgment of God as our sole provider. This realignment with the divine truth not only liberates us but also **protects our spiritual inheritance**.

The process of giving back what we gained from these covenants involves more than just a physical return; it requires a **legal and spiritual renunciation**, which effectively nullifies the claims these entities have over our lives. This action is not without its challenges. It can evoke fear of loss or uncertainty about the future. However, the **assurance of God's consistency and goodness** provides the strength to overcome these fears.

Scriptures like Hosea 2:1-13 not only illustrate the dangers of misattributed blessings but also outline the severe consequences of failing to rectify such errors. The narrative warns us about the **spiritual adultery of misattribution**, where blessings meant to be ascribed to God are wrongly credited to other sources, thereby granting demonic forces a foothold in our lives.

Through these scriptural insights, we are reminded of the **power of our testimony and the blood of Christ** which empower us to overcome the accuser. This victory is not just about personal liberation; it extends to our lineage, **securing a legacy of blessing untainted by demonic claims**.

Moreover, the act of giving back has profound implications for our spiritual authority. It's an exercise in humility and obedience, which strengthens our **spiritual jurisdiction and fortifies our defenses** against future spiritual encroachments.

By engaging in this spiritual housekeeping, we not only **ensure our own spiritual health** but also set a precedent for our descendants. In doing so, we **establish a legacy of purity and devotion** to God, ensuring that the blessings we enjoy and pass down are free from demonic taint.

. . .

REFLECTIVE QUESTIONS

1. What have you recognized as not from God in your life that needs to be given back?
2. How has the fear of loss affected your willingness to relinquish these gains?
3. In what ways have you experienced God's provision when you chose to trust Him over deceptive gains?
4. How can identifying the true source of your blessings change your spiritual outlook?
5. What steps can you take to ensure your legacy is free from demonic influences?

ACTIONABLE STEPS

1. **Cultivate a habit of discernment:** Regularly assess the sources of your blessings and gains. Pray for wisdom to discern gifts that are from God versus those that might entangle you with dark powers.
2. **Equip yourself with knowledge of the Word:** Deepen your understanding of scriptures related to God's provision and the spiritual laws concerning covenants and blessings. This knowledge will fortify your ability to stand firm in truth.
3. **Engage in spiritual housekeeping:** Make it a practice to regularly renounce and give back any gains identified as not from God. Use prayer and fasting as tools to cleanse your spiritual life.

JOURNALING Prompt

Reflect on any areas of your life where you might have accepted or held onto gains that were not from God. Consider the spiritual, emotional, and physical impacts of these gains. Journal about your process of giving them back and the outcomes you expect or hope to see from realigning with God's provisions.

~

CHAPTER 10

RETURNING ANYTHING GAINED!

Embrace the spiritual discipline of restitution as a powerful step towards liberation and divine alignment. When we willingly return what we have wrongfully gained, we make room for God's blessings that are rightfully ours.

James 4:7 Therefore submit to God. Resist the devil and he will flee from you.

Continuing from our previous discussion on the consequences of not relinquishing gains claimed by demonic entities, we delve into the remaining four potential outcomes. The process of **returning anything gained from demonic covenants** is not merely about detachment from ill-gotten gains but is a profound spiritual act of aligning with divine order and making room for legitimate blessings.

The fourth consequence we must be aware of is the **blocking of our paths to success.** When demonic claims are left unresolved, they can create spiritual barriers that prevent us from accessing the prosperity and success that God has outlined for us in His Word. This is vividly depicted in Hosea 2:6, where Israel's paths are hedged with thorns due to their allegiance to false sources of blessing. It is crucial to understand that spiritual legality can affect our physical reality, and the devil can use these legal footholds to impede our progress.

However, by meditating on and adhering to God's Word, as described in Joshua 1:8, we activate the promises of prosperity and success in our lives. This scripture not only promises success but outlines the condition—constant engagement with divine law. It became evident in my own journey that despite adherence to God's commands, unseen spiritual claims were hindering my breakthroughs. It was only through addressing these in the Courts of Heaven that the full manifestation of God's promise was realized.

When we truly **repent, renounce, and return** the gains as stated by demonic entities, we effectively dissolve the legal constraints they impose on us. This action reinstates our spiritual authority and reopens the pathways to divine prosperity and success, as God originally intended.

Another profound impact of unresolved demonic covenants is on our **social and spiritual reputation**. As witnessed in my own ministry, unresolved claims can lead to public misunderstandings and false accusations, which may stifle the growth and impact of our spiritual and social endeavors. This aligns with the teachings in Matthew 18:15-17, where Jesus outlines the approach to resolving personal grievances within the community. This directive not only helps in maintaining unity but also shields us from the spiritual repercussions of unresolved offenses that can give the devil a foothold.

The fifth consequence, as outlined in Hosea 2:8-9, is the **removal of prosperity**. When the true source of our blessings is not recognized or is falsely attributed to demonic influences, there is a spiritual dissonance that can lead to the withdrawal of these blessings. The devil exploits such misunderstandings to strip us of our prosperity, which is crucial not only for personal sustenance but for advancing God's kingdom on Earth as stated in Deuteronomy 8:18.

Prosperity in the kingdom context is not merely for personal consumption but is a strategic resource for the advancement of divine purposes across the globe. When legal rights are given to demonic entities through covenants, they aim to throttle the kingdom's advancement by cutting off the resources needed for its propagation.

The response to such challenges is a robust spiritual and practical re-engagement with the principles of God's kingdom. We must not only seek to annul these covenants but also to proactively engage in kingdom-building efforts that secure and extend our influence and resources in alignment with God's directives.

REFLECTIVE QUESTIONS

1. What barriers have you encountered that may be indicative of unresolved spiritual claims?
2. How can the act of returning wrongly gained blessings impact your spiritual journey?
3. What steps can you take to ensure your blessings are genuinely from God?
4. How can addressing spiritual legalities change your personal and ministry success?
5. In what ways can you apply the principles of restitution to resolve public misunderstandings and restore relationships?

ACTIONABLE STEPS

- **Cultivate transparency in your dealings:** Ensure that all your gains, whether material or spiritual, are acquired through righteous means. Regularly audit your life and ministry to safeguard against any gains that might give the enemy a foothold.
- **Equip yourself with scriptural knowledge:** Deepen your understanding of God's laws regarding blessings, covenants, and spiritual warfare. Use this knowledge to identify and sever any ungodly ties or covenants that may be affecting your life.
- **Engage in proactive restitution:** Wherever you identify gains that have not come through God's blessing, take swift action to return or renounce these. This act of obedience will realign you with God's purposes and open the doors to His legitimate blessings.

JOURNALING Prompt

Reflect on any aspects of your life where you might be holding onto gains that do not align with God's provisions. Consider the spiritual, emotional, and relational impacts of these gains. Journal about your journey towards restitution and the freedom you anticipate as you align more closely with God's will and His legitimate blessings.

~

CHAPTER II
INIQUITY UNDONE

Let us walk in the confidence that our God is greater than any ancestral sin. We are more than conquerors through Him who loves us, and by His grace, we can break every chain that seeks to bind our family's future.

"Blessed is the man to whom the Lord does not impute iniquity, And in whose spirit there is no deceit." - Psalm 32:2

In the spiritual journey of seeking freedom and fulfilling God's promises, we often encounter barriers that stem not just from our personal choices but from generational legacies. One such profound barrier is **iniquity**, a distortion that infiltrates family lines, creating predispositions toward specific sins. These are not merely personal failings but patterns embedded deep within our ancestry, shaping our spiritual and personal destinies in subtle yet significant ways. As believers, it's crucial to recognize and confront these patterns to achieve true liberation and spiritual health.

The concept of **iniquity** being **ancestral in nature** suggests that certain behaviors and tendencies are inherited, passed down through generations much like physical traits. This understanding is essential, for it frames our approach to spiritual healing—acknowledging that we are not just dealing with isolated behaviors but with deep-rooted spiritual legacies. The legal basis for such claims against us, as highlighted by Exodus 20:4-5, provides a clear boundary for these influences, affecting up to four generations. This scriptural insight establishes a legal framework within which we can operate to address and nullify these claims.

Addressing iniquities involves more than personal repentance; it requires a legal confrontation in the spiritual realm, specifically in the Courts of Heaven. This venue serves as a platform where believers can dispute the accusations Satan leverages against them due to the sins of their forebearers. **The role of the Courts of Heaven** is pivotal in this process, as it allows for the presentation and dismissal of claims based on the bloodline sins that might be hindering our spiritual progress and the fulfillment of God's promises.

When we **understand the impact of iniquity on personal destiny**, we realize why many remain trapped in cycles of frustration and defeat despite earnest spiritual efforts. These cycles are often manifestations of unresolved spiritual legacies. Engaging in this battle requires knowledge, prayer, and the active renouncing of ties that bind us to past iniquities. Through repentance for these ancestral sins, we can break the legal rights that these iniquities hold over us, thereby releasing us and our future generations from their grip.

The journey towards resolving these issues is marked by several crucial steps. Firstly, identifying the **specific nature of the ancestral sins** is fundamental. This involves seeking revelation through prayer, meditation, and sometimes through genealogical research. Once identified, the next step is **repenting**

on behalf of our bloodline, which helps in revoking the rights these iniquities have over our lives. This act of repentance is not just about turning away from sin; it's about realigning our family's spiritual legacy towards righteousness.

Practical steps for addressing iniquities include regular spiritual check-ups where we assess not only our actions but also our inherent tendencies that might be influenced by our family history. These check-ups should be coupled with a deliberate and informed approach to prayer that targets these specific issues. Additionally, cultivating a lifestyle that consistently opposes these ancestral sins can help fortify our spiritual defenses against them.

The freedom achieved through resolving these spiritual issues is profound. It not only impacts our spiritual health but also ensures that our descendants will not have to battle the same spiritual enemies again. This process of cleansing our bloodline from iniquities is therefore not just about us—it's about setting a course for generational blessings and establishing a **legacy of righteousness**.

To maintain this newfound freedom, **continuous vigilance against iniquity** is essential. We must remain proactive in guarding against the re-establishment of these old patterns in our lives and in the lives of our children. This ongoing battle requires dedication to spiritual disciplines such as prayer, fasting, and the study of the Word, which equip us to stand firm against any resurgence of these issues.

In conclusion, dealing with iniquities in our bloodline is a powerful step toward personal and generational freedom. It allows us to step into the fullness of what God has planned for us, free from the shackles of our past. By understanding and applying these principles, we can navigate our spiritual journey with greater clarity and effectiveness, ensuring that our legacy is one of blessings, not burdens.

. . .

REFLECTIVE QUESTIONS

1. **What specific patterns of sin are prevalent in your family history**, and how might they be influencing your current spiritual and personal life?
2. **How does the concept of iniquity shape your understanding of personal sin** and its impact on your family?
3. **What steps can you take to uncover hidden iniquities** within your bloodline?
4. **How can you practically apply the principles of the Courts of Heaven** to address ancestral sins?
5. **In what ways can you cultivate a lifestyle** that actively opposes ancestral iniquities?

ACTIONABLE STEPS

- **Cultivate**: Establish a daily prayer routine that focuses on seeking revelation about and healing from ancestral sins.
- **Equip**: Study and meditate on scriptures related to deliverance from iniquity, such as Psalm 51 and Psalm 32, to equip yourself with the knowledge needed to break free from generational curses.
- **Engage**: Engage in a community of believers who understand and support your journey towards freedom from ancestral sins, providing accountability and encouragement.

Journaling Prompt

Reflect on any known ancestral sins in your family and consider how they might have shaped the patterns in your life. Write about your commitment to breaking these cycles and the steps you plan to take to achieve this freedom.

CHAPTER 12

INIQUITY INTERRUPTION OF GOD'S WILL

As we walk through life, let us be reminded that God has not left us powerless against the forces that seek to shape our destiny contrary to His will. In Christ, we have the authority to confront and overcome any iniquitous influences inherited from our forebears, ensuring our path aligns with the divine purpose and grace given to us before time began.

"For we do not wrestle against flesh and blood, but against principalities, against powers, against the rulers of the darkness of this age, against spiritual hosts of wickedness in the heavenly places." - Ephesians 6:12 NKJV

In exploring **Iniquity: Interruption of God's Will**, we delve into how iniquity, if left unaddressed, can subtly dictate the course of our lives. This chapter sheds light on the **powerful impact of ancestral iniquity** and the ongoing battle between the divine blueprint inscribed in our heavenly books and the blemishes of our lineage. Recognizing these forces is the first step towards claiming the life preordained for us in the heavens.

The central theme revolves around the **heavenly books** that chronicle our divine purpose and the grace meant to propel us towards our destiny. Understanding that these books contain the blueprint of our lives underscores the importance of ensuring they are not only recognized but also actively contended for in the Courts of Heaven.

Addressing iniquity in the **Courts of Heaven** is pivotal for realigning our life's trajectory with God's original design. By legally challenging the claims of iniquity through spiritual litigation, we reclaim our heritage and initiate a legacy of blessing and divine fulfillment.

The act of **worship** plays a crucial role in accessing and activating the prophetic destiny laid out in our heavenly books. Through true worship, we unlock the spiritual realm, allowing us to receive revelation and insight into our purpose and the strategies needed to fulfill it.

By understanding and engaging with the **legal spiritual framework** provided by the Courts of Heaven, we empower ourselves to dismantle generational curses and establish generational blessings. This legal approach not only changes our lives but also sets a precedent for those who follow, altering the spiritual landscape for future generations.

The **opening of our prophetic books** is essential for receiving revelation about our divine assignments. If these books remain sealed, we wander without direction, susceptible to the whims of iniquity and devoid of prophetic insight. Engaging in genuine worship and spiritual warfare is vital to unlocking these books.

Prophetic discernment enables us to navigate our spiritual journey with clarity and purpose. By understanding what is written in our heavenly books, we can actively pursue our God-given destiny, turning potential into reality and ensuring that our lives reflect God's ultimate plan for us.

Through the **judicial processes of the heavenly court**, we are able to challenge the adversary's claims legally and reclaim our spiritual heritage. This judicial engagement ensures that our spiritual journey is not dictated by our past but shaped by our divine future.

As we **cultivate a lifestyle of worship and spiritual engagement**, we keep our heavenly books open and our lives aligned with God's purposes. This alignment allows us to live out our days as intended, marked by divine guidance and fulfillment.

REFLECTIVE QUESTIONS

1. How might unresolved iniquity be influencing your current spiritual and life challenges?
2. What steps can you take to learn more about the heavenly books and your divine purpose as noted in them?
3. How can you incorporate more authentic worship into your daily routine to ensure your heavenly books remain open?
4. What does it mean to you to legally contend for your divine destiny in the Courts of Heaven?
5. How can engaging with the Courts of Heaven change your perspective on spiritual warfare and intercession?

ACTIONABLE STEPS

- **Cultivate a deeper understanding** of your spiritual heritage and the biblical basis for heavenly books through study and meditation.
- **Equip yourself with knowledge** on the dynamics of the Courts of Heaven and how to effectively present your case against iniquitous claims.
- **Engage in regular, deliberate acts of worship** that align your spirit with God's presence and open up the channels for prophetic revelation.

JOURNALING Prompt

Consider the areas of your life where you might be experiencing the effects of ancestral iniquity. Reflect on how understanding your heavenly books and engaging in the Courts of Heaven could transform these areas. Write down specific steps you plan to take to deepen your engagement with these spiritual tools.

CHAPTER 13

THE FOUR PURPOSES OF INIQUITY

God's power is greater than any inherited weakness or failure in our bloodline. Through His grace, we can break the strongholds of iniquity and walk fully in the purpose He has destined for us.

"For You, O Lord, will bless the righteous; with favor You will surround him as with a shield." – Psalm 5:12 NKJV

In this chapter, we uncover the **four main purposes of iniquity** and how it seeks to interfere with God's divine will in our lives. Iniquity, left unresolved, grants satan the **legal right to resist God's plans** for us, affecting areas like temptation, identity, destiny, and even building cases against us in the Courts of Heaven. It is critical to understand these dynamics to annul their effects and secure our God-given destiny.

First, iniquity gives the **right to tempt us in specific areas.** The enemy uses iniquity as a foundation to entice us through inherited weaknesses or proclivities, creating patterns of sin. James 1:13-15 reveals that we are tempted by our desires, which are often shaped by the iniquity in our bloodline. When we yield to these temptations, the devil builds a legal case against us, perpetuating a destructive cycle.

Secondly, **iniquity fashions our identity** by distorting how we view ourselves. Iniquity can cause us to internalize shame, guilt, or unworthiness, robbing us of the confidence to embrace who God has called us to be. Isaiah's transformation in Isaiah 6 shows that when iniquity is removed, our true identity in Christ is revealed.

The third purpose of iniquity is to **destroy destinies.** By influencing decisions and behaviors, iniquity can lead us down paths of destruction rather than the destiny outlined in our heavenly books. This is evident in the example of family curses and personal choices shaped by unaddressed iniquity. However, choosing to align with God can break these destructive cycles.

Finally, **iniquity builds cases against us in the Courts of Heaven.** Satan uses broken covenants and sins in our bloodline as legal arguments to hinder blessings and bring famine or lack. The story of David addressing Saul's breach of a covenant with the Gibeonites highlights how unresolved iniquity can affect an entire generation. Yet through repentance and restitution, we can break these legal claims and restore God's blessings.

Addressing iniquity requires spiritual diligence and humility. Through repentance, worship, and engaging with the Courts of Heaven, we can revoke the enemy's rights and fully align with God's will.

REFLECTIVE QUESTIONS

1. What patterns or struggles in your life might be connected to iniquity in your bloodline?

2. How can the removal of iniquity transform your sense of identity and purpose?
3. Have there been broken covenants in your life or family history that need repentance?
4. What steps can you take to actively address and annul the effects of iniquity in your life?
5. How does the example of Peter's restoration encourage you to trust God with your destiny?

ACTIONABLE STEPS

- **Cultivate repentance** by asking God to reveal any areas where iniquity may have influence and sincerely seeking His forgiveness.
- **Equip yourself with knowledge** about the Courts of Heaven and the biblical principles of repentance and restitution.
- **Engage in consistent worship and prayer** to open the heavenly books and align yourself with God's purpose for your life.

JOURNALING Prompt

Reflect on any recurring struggles or patterns in your life that may stem from iniquity in your bloodline. How can understanding God's grace and engaging in spiritual warfare help you break free from these cycles? Write down a prayer of repentance and a declaration of your commitment to walk fully in God's will.

OPERATING IN THE COURTS OF HEAVEN TO CLEANSE YOU...

CHAPTER 14
SILENCING VOICES

The voices in the spirit realm must be silenced for God's plans to manifest fully in our lives. When accusations from the enemy are nullified, the power of God's kingdom is free to flow in and through us.

"No weapon formed against you shall prosper, and every tongue which rises against you in judgment you shall condemn. This is the heritage of the servants of the Lord, and their righteousness is from Me," says the Lord. – Isaiah 54:17 NKJV

In this chapter, we learn the critical importance of **silencing voices in the spirit realm** that oppose us. These voices, as Revelation 12:10-11 describes, are accusations brought by the enemy before God. The accuser works tirelessly, day and night, to bring legal claims against us using the sins of our past, personal actions, and the iniquities of our bloodlines. His accusations aim to hinder the manifestation of God's kingdom in our lives.

When we understand that **these accusations are legal arguments in the Courts of Heaven**, it becomes clear that silencing them is not just about combating physical or emotional attacks but targeting their spiritual origins. Isaiah 54:17 teaches that **it is the tongues rising in judgment against us that create weapons** in the spiritual realm. These tongues must be condemned in the Courts of Heaven. By using the authority given to us through Christ, we can nullify the words of the accuser and stop their power to influence our lives.

The **blood of Jesus is our ultimate testimony** in the Courts of Heaven. It speaks on our behalf, silencing the voices that accuse us. When we align our prayers with the testimony of the blood, we actively participate in nullifying accusations. Jesus' sacrifice on the cross legally defeated the enemy, but we must claim that victory in the Courts of Heaven by presenting our case and agreeing with the power of His blood.

It is also essential to recognize that **our righteousness is a gift from God**. This righteousness gives us the authority to condemn accusations and nullify the enemy's claims. Romans 5:17 reminds us that we reign in life through the abundance of grace and the gift of righteousness. This inheritance, our spiritual birthright, empowers us to stand boldly in the Courts of Heaven and silence voices that attempt to hinder our destinies.

Furthermore, silencing these voices is a **key step in cleansing our bloodline**. Iniquities in our bloodline often provide the enemy with material to accuse us. By addressing these iniquities and bringing them under the cleansing power of Jesus' blood, we break the legal grounds for accusations. This act not only frees us but also transforms the spiritual inheritance of our descendants.

Operating in the Courts of Heaven requires faith, understanding, and humility. As we present our case, we remind the Courts of our covenant with God and stand on the authority granted through Christ's righteousness. With this confidence, we can boldly declare that every voice speaking against us is illegal and unrighteous. This process not only silences the accuser but also leads to breakthroughs in areas where we have faced resistance.

By silencing these voices, we experience a shift in the spiritual atmosphere. Weapons formed against us lose their power because the voices empowering them are nullified. This opens the way for God's kingdom to manifest fully in our lives, bringing freedom, restoration, and the fulfillment of His promises.

REFLECTIVE QUESTIONS

1. What voices or accusations do you sense are working against you spiritually?
2. How can understanding the Courts of Heaven change the way you approach spiritual warfare?
3. What steps have you taken to address iniquities in your bloodline and silence accusations tied to them?
4. How does the righteousness of Christ empower you to condemn accusations in the spiritual realm?
5. In what areas of your life have you seen breakthroughs after silencing accusations through prayer?

ACTIONABLE STEPS

- **Cultivate a deeper understanding** of the spiritual realm by studying scriptures about the Courts of Heaven and the power of Jesus' blood.

- **Equip yourself with spiritual authority** by affirming your righteousness in Christ and standing on God's promises in prayer.
- **Engage in targeted intercession** to silence accusations in the spiritual realm, addressing specific areas where the enemy has legal grounds.

JOURNALING **Prompt**

Reflect on any areas in your life where you feel stuck or hindered. Ask God to reveal if there are accusations or voices in the spirit realm working against you. Write a prayer of repentance, aligning yourself with the testimony of Jesus' blood, and declare those voices silenced in the Courts of Heaven. Document any insights or breakthroughs you experience.

CHAPTER 15

SIGNS OF CURSES FROM OUR BLOODLINE

When it feels like life is pressing against you from all sides, remember that no curse can operate in your life without a cause. God's Word assures us that He has given us authority to break free from the oppressive patterns of curses. By addressing the spiritual and legal roots of these forces, you can experience the fullness of God's blessings and live in victory. Be encouraged that God's promises are sure, and His power is greater than any force working against you.

"No weapon formed against you shall prosper, and every tongue which rises against you in judgment You shall condemn. This is the heritage of the servants of the Lord, and their righteousness is from Me," says the Lord." Isaiah 54:17

Curses are not random forces but spiritual powers requiring a legal right to operate. **Curses require a legal cause to operate**, often rooted in unresolved issues from our bloodline, much like a bird searching for a place to land. Understanding this principle enables us to remove their legal rights and revoke their power. When curses find a foothold, their effect is to **weaken us spiritually**, just as Balak sought to weaken Israel by hiring Balaam to curse them. Without this weakening force, the enemy knows we are more than conquerors through Christ, and he will use curses to diminish our spiritual authority.

Another hallmark of curses is **repetitive attacks**. If it seems like you are facing one crisis after another without relief, this could signify a curse working against you. This was my experience during a season of unrelenting opposition. The spiritual floodwaters were overwhelming until I addressed the root cause. Once dealt with, the attacks stopped, and peace returned. Adding to this, **curses are aggressive and persistent**, chasing us down like the curses described in Deuteronomy 28. They will pursue, overtake, and attempt to destroy unless we address their root cause. The story of Jericho's cursed waters is a vivid illustration of this truth.

In many cases, **prayer seems ineffective against curses** because they operate within the legal systems of heaven. It wasn't until I discovered the Courts of Heaven that I began to understand how to break these curses by addressing their legal claims. **Bloodline issues often fuel curses**, as ancestral sins provide the enemy with grounds to accuse us. Unresolved iniquities in our history become a foothold for curses to take root and sabotage our lives.

The impact of curses can be devastating, often manifesting as **miscarriage, barrenness, and loss**. Like Jericho, even pleasant places can be overshadowed by a curse that disrupts life and productivity. This aggression from curses is relentless, and **persistent misfortune**—patterns of repeated failure despite best efforts—may signal their presence. Recognizing these patterns allows us to seek their removal. Living under such oppression can lead to **weariness and fatigue**, a heaviness that drains spiritual and physical energy. Breaking the curse brings restoration and vitality.

The ultimate breakthrough comes when we recognize that **curses are nullified through legal action in the Courts of Heaven**. By applying the blood of Jesus and presenting our case before the Righteous Judge, we revoke the enemy's right to oppress us. This process restores us to the blessings and purposes God has intended for us, replacing the destructive effects of curses with divine favor and freedom.

REFLECTIVE QUESTIONS

1. What patterns or challenges in your life might indicate a curse operating through your bloodline?
2. How does understanding the legal nature of curses change your perspective on dealing with spiritual opposition?
3. What role does prayer play in identifying and breaking curses, and how does the revelation of the Courts of Heaven enhance this process?
4. Can you identify areas of your life where persistent misfortune or weariness might signify unresolved spiritual issues?
5. How does the authority of Jesus and the power of His blood equip you to break free from curses and walk in blessing?

ACTIONABLE STEPS

- **Cultivate** a habit of examining your life and family history for patterns that may suggest unresolved iniquity or curses. Ask the Holy Spirit to bring revelation.
- **Equip** yourself with the knowledge of God's Word about spiritual authority and the power of the blood of Jesus to break curses and revoke legal rights in the Courts of Heaven.
- **Engage** in intentional prayer, bringing these issues before God as Judge, and ask for His verdict to nullify any legal rights that curses may have over you or your family.

JOURNALING Prompt

Reflect on areas of persistent struggle or failure in your life. Write about possible connections to unresolved issues in your bloodline and how you can partner with God to address these through prayer and spiritual authority. Document specific prayers and breakthroughs as you bring these matters before the Courts of Heaven.

CHAPTER 16

THE CURSE OF PREMATURE DEATH

When it seems like the promises of God for long and satisfying life are being thwarted, take heart that through the redemptive work of Jesus Christ, every curse can be broken. God desires to satisfy you with long life and reveal His salvation. Even when curses seem rooted in generations past, His power to redeem and restore is greater. Trust in His love, grace, and faithfulness as you seek to silence every voice and legal right working against His plans for your life.

"With long life I will satisfy him, and show him My salvation." Psalm 91:16

The curse of premature death is one of the most devastating attacks that can operate against a person or family. **Curses require a legal cause to operate**, and the shedding of innocent blood—whether through murder or abortion—provides one such cause. This opens the door for the enemy to land curses on a bloodline. However, God's promise is for a long and satisfying life, filled with His protection and salvation, as seen in Psalm 91.

Another significant cause of this curse is **sins unto death**, which can lead either to spiritual separation from God or physical consequences. The apostle Paul addressed **the dangers of taking communion in an unworthy manner**, highlighting that failure to discern the Lord's body brought weakness, sickness, and even death. It is critical to approach the Lord's Supper with reverence and proper understanding. Similarly, **dishonoring prophetic voices** can incur curses, as seen in Abimelech's interaction with Abraham. Honoring those God sends into our lives protects us and preserves generational blessings.

Scripture also warns us against **treating God as common**, an error that can result in severe consequences. The sons of Aaron, Ananias and Sapphira, and others who disregarded the holiness of God faced judgments that brought premature death. **Presumption before the Lord**, whether through careless actions or unbridled ambition in the supernatural realm, creates openings for the enemy. The strange fire offered by Nadab and Abihu and the presumption of self-proclaimed prophets demonstrate the serious nature of stepping outside God's directives.

Finally, the sin of **familiarity with holy things** can bring unintended consequences. Uzzah's death after touching the ark of the covenant reflects the dangers of becoming casual with God's sacred presence. These patterns—whether they involve individual actions or bloodline sins—allow the enemy to enforce curses unless addressed through repentance and legal annulment in the Courts of Heaven. By acknowledging and repenting for these areas, we can revoke the enemy's claims and walk in the fullness of God's promises.

REFLECTIVE QUESTIONS

1. Have you noticed patterns of premature death or shortened lifespans in your family history that might indicate unresolved bloodline issues?
2. What steps can you take to ensure that you approach the Lord's Supper with reverence and discernment?
3. How can honoring God's prophetic voices and His presence in your life protect you from spiritual and physical harm?
4. In what ways might presumption or familiarity with holy things manifest in your actions or beliefs, and how can you address these areas?
5. How can you intentionally apply the promise of Psalm 91:16 to counteract any fear or doubt about living a long and satisfying life?

ACTIONABLE STEPS

- **Cultivate** a reverence for the holiness of God by intentionally reflecting on His attributes and His work in your life.
- **Equip** yourself with knowledge of scripture regarding the power of repentance and God's promises for a long life, such as Psalm 91:16.
- **Engage** in intentional repentance for any personal or bloodline sins, asking God to revoke the enemy's legal rights in the Courts of Heaven.

JOURNALING Prompt

Reflect on areas where curses of premature death may have influenced your family or personal life. Write a prayer of repentance and commitment, asking God to break every curse and replace it with His promise of long and satisfying life. Document any specific insights or breakthroughs you experience as you address these areas with Him.

CHAPTER 17

REVOKING CURSES THAT SHORTEN LIFESPANS

When faced with the curse of a shortened lifespan, be encouraged that through repentance, faith, and the power of Jesus' blood, we can revoke every legal right of the enemy. God's promise of long and satisfying life is assured for His covenant people. By addressing areas of rebellion, dishonor, and foolishness, and aligning ourselves with His holiness, we open the way for the fullness of His promises to manifest in our lives.

"With long life I will satisfy him, and show him My salvation." Psalm 91:16

The Bible offers clear guidance on **revoking curses that cause premature death** by addressing their roots. One significant cause is **rebellion against God's authority**, exemplified by Korah's defiance in Numbers 16. Rebellion creates an opening for untimely death as it resists God's established order. Scripture calls us to submit to governing authorities as part of our submission to God. Rebellion, whether in our own lives or in our bloodlines, grants the enemy legal claims that must be addressed through repentance.

Parents also hold an essential role in securing their children's futures. **Correcting children in love protects them from legal claims of the enemy**, as Proverbs 23:13 assures. Discipline removes tendencies that invite destructive behavior and aligns children with God's design for their lives. Similarly, **honoring parents is foundational to the promise of long life and success**, as emphasized in Ephesians 6. This principle applies not only during childhood but throughout our lives. Even when parents fail in their actions, we are called to honor their position, acknowledging that without them, we would not exist. Dishonor gives the enemy access to attack us and our lineage.

Wickedness and foolishness can also shorten lifespans, as stated in Ecclesiastes 7:17. These open doors for the enemy to operate in the Courts of Heaven. Foolishness, often expressed through careless and excessive words, carries weight in the spiritual realm. Jesus warned that every idle word is accounted for in the day of judgment. Being intentional and measured in our speech closes gaps the enemy could exploit.

Scripture also teaches us to **treat God as holy and not common**, as seen in the consequences faced by Uzzah and others who failed to honor His presence. Profane fire, rebellion, and presumption invite consequences, but reverence and humility safeguard us. In all these matters, God is not the author of these curses. Instead, the enemy takes advantage of rebellion, dishonor, or foolishness in us or our bloodlines to land premature death. Through repentance and the redemptive work of Christ, we can revoke every legal claim and walk in the promise of a long and satisfying life.

REFLECTIVE QUESTIONS

1. What areas of rebellion—whether personal or in your bloodline—might be granting the enemy access to premature death in your life?
2. How can you ensure that you correct your children in a way that aligns them with God's purposes and protects their future?
3. In what ways can you honor your parents, even when their actions have been imperfect or harmful?
4. How can you intentionally guard your speech to avoid opening doors for the enemy in the Courts of Heaven?
5. What steps can you take to approach God with greater reverence and honor His presence in your daily life?

ACTIONABLE STEPS

- **Cultivate** an attitude of submission to God's authority and those He has placed in leadership, ensuring rebellion has no place in your heart.
- **Equip** yourself with an understanding of biblical principles for discipline, honor, and reverence, applying these in your relationships and daily actions.
- **Engage** in prayer and repentance for areas of rebellion, dishonor, or foolishness in your life and bloodline, asking God to revoke the enemy's legal claims.

. . .

JOURNALING Prompt

Reflect on the areas of your life where curses of shortened lifespans may be operating, whether through rebellion, dishonor, or careless words. Write a prayer of repentance, committing to honoring God's authority, correcting your speech, and treating His presence with reverence. Document any insights or breakthroughs as you address these areas with the Lord.

CHAPTER 18

FROM DEFENDANT TO JUDGE

When we address the iniquities and covenants within our bloodlines, we step into a transformative realm of authority in the Courts of Heaven. God calls us not only to be cleansed but to take on the role of judges in His divine judicial system. This is an invitation to rise from the position of one who pleads for mercy to one who exercises justice. Through the righteousness imparted by Jesus' blood, we are empowered to represent ourselves, our families, and even our nations, securing the blessings of heaven.

"If you will walk in My ways, and if you will keep My command, then you shall also judge My house, and likewise have charge of My courts; I will give you places to walk among these who stand here." Zechariah 3:7

Joshua the high priest's story illustrates the **journey from defendant to judge**. Initially, he stood before the Courts of Heaven wearing filthy garments, symbolic of **iniquity in his bloodline**. This iniquity allowed Satan to oppose him and hinder his priestly duties. When the Lord removed these filthy garments, declaring, "See, I have removed your iniquity," Joshua was cleansed and robed in righteousness. This transformation positioned him to judge God's house and oversee the Courts, showing that addressing bloodline issues unlocks higher realms of spiritual authority.

As kings and priests to our God, we are called to this dual role. **Being washed in Jesus' blood qualifies us for positions of spiritual authority**, enabling us to present cases in heaven and release God's decrees on earth. Revelation 1 confirms this identity, empowering us to secure blessings for ourselves, our families, and the cultures we influence. Judgeship in the Courts of Heaven is not reserved for a select few; it is available to all who allow God to cleanse and equip them.

Daniel 7 reveals the **heavenly judicial system as a panel of judges** presided over by the Ancient of Days. Thrones are set for those qualified to sit upon them. Just as Joshua transitioned from wearing filthy garments to occupying a seat of authority, we too are invited to take our place in God's divine order. This transition is pivotal; we move from merely defending against accusations to actively executing justice and securing blessings.

The removal of iniquity in our lives allows us to step into the **judicial order of heaven**. As judges, we gain the authority to represent nations, cultures, and generations before God. The work of Jesus on the cross is sufficient to cleanse us completely, enabling us to fulfill this high calling. In this position, we do not act out of our own merit but through the grace and righteousness imparted by Christ.

REFLECTIVE QUESTIONS

1. What iniquities or covenants in your bloodline might still be hindering your ability to walk fully in your spiritual authority?
2. How can you actively embrace your identity as both king and priest in God's kingdom?
3. What steps can you take to transition from pleading as a defendant to operating as a judge in the Courts of Heaven?
4. In what ways can you represent your family, culture, or nation before God's judicial system?
5. How does the removal of iniquity transform your perspective on spiritual authority and your role in advancing God's kingdom?

ACTIONABLE STEPS

- **Cultivate** a deeper understanding of your identity in Christ as both a king and priest, ensuring that you walk in the authority granted by His blood.
- **Equip** yourself through prayer and study to address and repent of any remaining iniquities or covenants in your bloodline that hinder your spiritual role.
- **Engage** actively in representing your family, culture, or nation in the Courts of Heaven, decreeing God's blessings and securing His will on earth.

JOURNALING **Prompt**

Reflect on the areas of your life where you feel opposition or limitation in fulfilling your spiritual calling. Write a prayer of repentance for iniquities or covenants in your bloodline and document your thoughts on transitioning from a defendant to a judge in the Courts of Heaven. Record any insights you receive about representing your family, culture, or nation before God.

D DESTINY IMAGE

Destiny Image is a prophetic Christian publisher dedicated to empowering believers through Spirit-led messages. Our mission is to equip and inspire individuals to fulfill their God-given destinies by providing transformative resources that resonate with the Charismatic and Pentecostal faith.

We specialize in books, blogs, and back cover copies that reflect prophetic insights, dynamic teachings, and testimonies of faith. Our commitment to fostering spiritual growth and kingdom impact makes Destiny Image a beacon for those seeking to deepen their relationship with God and embrace their calling in the power of the Holy Spirit.